The Little Book
of Outd

Ideas for outdoor activities for the Early Years Foundation Stage

by Sally Featherstone

Illustrations by
Kerry Ingham

Little Books with **BIG** ideas®

The Little Book of Outdoor Play

ISBN 1-902233-74-3
978-1-902233-74-3-1

©Featherstone Education Ltd, 2007
Text © Sally Featherstone, 2001
Illustrations © Kerry Ingham, 2005
Series Editor, Sally Featherstone

First published in the UK, August 2001

'Little Books' is a trade mark of Featherstone Education Ltd

Published in the United Kingdom by
Featherstone Education Ltd
44 - 46 High Street
Husbands Bosworth
Leicestershire
LE17 6LP

This book is dedicated to the staff of
Battledown Children's Centre, Cheltenham,
who suggested that I should write down some
of the ideas we shared during a day
in their garden.

Sally Featherstone
July 2001

The Little Book of Outdoor Play

Outdoor Play

Outside play is an entitlement for all children in the Early Years Foundation Stage. In our society, anxiety about children's safety and the increasingly sedentary nature of family life means that children may grow up with few opportunities to play outdoors. Many have no contact with their friends at the end of the day or at weekends. Playing in the garden or the park is an unfamiliar concept to many, and extended periods of uninterrupted physical activity are rare, even inside our settings.

Outdoor play should not just consist of what I heard described as "batting about on bikes." It is not just more playtime - using the playground after the older children have finished with it. It is a planned part of children's experiences.

The Guidance for the Early Years Foundation stage states that

"Practitioners should

* Plan activities which offer appropriate physical challenges
* Provide sufficient space, indoors and outdoors to set up relevant activities
* Give sufficient time for children to use a range of equipment
* Provide resources that can be used in a variety of ways or to support specific skills
* Introduce the language of movement alongside their actions
* Use additional adult help to support individuals and to encourage increased independence in physical activities"

In some settings it is possible for children to have unrestricted access to outside play with their friends; play which gives those appropriate challenges, with space and time to develop their ideas, good resources and supportive adults. Poor access, shared spaces, vandalism or safety may all be reasons for limiting access to fresh air and space to move freely. However, these reasons should not become excuses for neglecting the contribution that the outside environment can make to children's experiences in the Early Years Foundation Stage and beyond.

Outdoor play should present all the possibilities of the best garden. A garden with many friends to play with and more possibilities than you can imagine. It should excite the senses, involve all the muscles, stimulate the imagination. Anything that can be done inside can be done outside, and so much more. Children can make more mess, more noise, more speed and more size in a garden. With a bit of imagination and organisation of resources even the smallest, least promising area can be transformed into an exciting place to be.

6

Links with the Early Learning Goals for the Early Years Foundation Stage

The Early Learning Goals which are particularly relevant to outdoor play are:

Personal and social development

- Continue to be interested, excited and motivated to learn
- Respond to significant experiences, showing a range of feelings when appropriate
- Work as part of a group or class, taking turns and sharing fairly, understanding that there need to be agreed values and codes of behaviour for groups of people, including adults and children, to work together harmoniously
- Select and use activities and resources independently

Language, communication and literacy

- Use language to imagine and recreate roles and experiences
- Interact with others, negotiating plans and activities and taking turns in conversations
- Attempt writing for various purposes, using features of different forms such as lists, stories, instructions
- Write their own names and labels and form sentences, some-times using punctuation

Problem Solving, Reasoning and Numeracy

- Use everyday words to describe position

Knowledge and Understanding of the World

- Find out about, and identify some features of living things, objects and events they observe
- Ask questions about why things happen and how things work
- Build and construct with a wide range of objects, selecting appropriate resources and adapting their work where necessary

- Observe, find out and identify features in the place they live and the natural world

Physical Development

- Move with confidence, imagination and with safety
- Move with control and co-ordination
- Show awareness of space, themselves and others
- Use a range of small and large equipment
- Travel around, under, over and through balancing and climbing equipment

Contents

Focus of the page	page number
Shelters	10 and 11
Surfaces	12 and 13
Textures	14 and 15
Marks and markings	16 and 17
Boundaries and dividers	18 and 19
Gardening	20 and 21
Weather	22 and 23
Art in the garden	24 and 25
Animals and minibeasts	26 and 27
Writing outside	28 and 29
Sounds and music	30 and 31
Construction	32 and 33
Quiet areas	34 and 35
Role play in the garden	36 and 37
Surprises	38 and 39
Small apparatus	40 and 41
More permanent structures	42 and 43
Access for all children	44 and 45
More shelters, structures and dividers	48 and 49
Flowering plants for your garden	50 and 51
Shrubs for your garden	52
Indoor plants for children to grow	53
Food plants and plants to attract butterflies and other insects	54

Shelters

Shelters provide security and a sense of fun. You can make them quickly with pegs, poles, bamboo canes, elastic tied around posts or fixed apparatus.

Use thin material for temporary shelters, so it can be secured by pegs or elastic. Use trees and fences to provide support for leaning sheets of card. Tie a rope round two uprights and hang a blanket over the rope to provide a classic tent.

If you want something more permanent, look in garden centres for gazebos, parasols, play houses, sheds and awnings. Look for sale prices at the end of summer.

Put up battens so you can suspend fabric or wood across corners or along walls to provide shade and protection from sun or the occasional shower.

Don't forget to add signs, notices and labels. Add small baskets of materials and equipment to stimulate play.

Pop ups

Pop up tents are cheap and easy to erect. They come in several sizes and provide quick and easy hiding places and role play bases. Get them from early years catalogues or toyshops. A notice or sign will focus the play, a sleeping bag inside will add a new dimension.

Boxes

Carboard or wooden boxes are often free. Cut holes in the sides for windows and doors. Paint them if you like (put glue in the paint to make them showerproof). Make boats, houses, spaceships, submarines. Take them apart and use the big sheets to make structures and walls.*

Huts & sheds

When all the toys are out, use your shed for a role play corner or garage. You could put a table across the doorway to make a counter for a shop or cafe.

Tents

If you have grass, pitch a real tent and peg it down. Or you could use a frame tent and weight it with bricks. Pairs of little tents make extra fun.

Awnings

Fix a wooden batten to the wall, at about head height. Then you can pin or tape a fabric awning to it and tie the ends to two poles. Make the shelter into a shop or use it to provide shade for table top games, books, sand or bricks.

Poles & screening

Set some broom handles in buckets or big tins of concrete, When the concrete has set, use two or more to make screens by clipping or nailing trellis, fabric, card, bamboo screening, plastic sheet or hardboard to the broom handles.

Surfaces

Asphalt or concrete is weatherproof and hardwearing but we can extend children's experiences of textures on surfaces by some imaginative thinking.

Your existing surfaces could be enhanced by painting them (perhaps with glitter, sand or sawdust added to the paint).

Grass can be allowed to grow long in some places to provide flowers and minibeasts.

Lift an occasional paving stone to provide space for growing things or inset matting, rubber or metal sheet.

Put some texture on the walls by adding tiles, sticking objects on or painting some of the bricks.

Astro-turf or even some carpets can provide a water-proof and all weather surface outside.

Decking is good value and provides quick coverage.

Natural

Encourage moss to grow between cracks or on surfaces. Coating things with plain yogurt helps moss and lichens to grow.
Try growing grass on the top of a wall, lift some pavings and add turf, sow camomile or wildflowers.

Inside outside

Take a piece of carpet (or some carpet tiles or carpet samples) outside. Put a piece of lino or vinyl flooring under the sand tray. Try cork tiles where the area is protected. Bring playmats outside in all weathers, they dry quickly.

Loose surfaces

Cover mud or bare patches with gravel or chippings. Bark is nice to walk on, but be careful: it may attract local wildlife - or dogs!

Patterns

Cobbles, sand, little stones, mosaics and slices of wood can all be made into patterns on the ground. Use them singly, or combine them to make a collage.

Walls & fences

If you have a kiln or self hardening clay, make some tiles with the children. Make hand prints and stencils with thick paint, and spray with varnish to protect. Use mosaic pieces or small stones to construct patterns in quick drying cement or plaster.

Wood & metal

Children's pictures on wood can be hung on a wall for a gallery. Plywood and hard-board need to be well sealed. Metal sheet, mirror tiles, metal objects set in plaster, coins, counters and old wooden bricks all provide surface interest.

Textures

Providing textures in play situations extends children's opportunities to explore a wide range of natural and man made materials. Many children play exclusively with plastic toys and man made materials. Offering other textures will expand their experience and with it their language and vocabulary.

Provide textures for looking at, touching, walking on, blowing, wrapping yourself in, tossing, squeezing and stretching.

Try collecting a range of different textured materials and objects - ask parents to help with this. Then dip into your collection and hang, wrap, spread, cover, line, tip, shake, sort and discuss what things feel like to hands, feet, faces, noses as children handle the ones you offer or choose their own from a basket or box.

Hang it

Try hanging things from trees, ropes, doorways, fixed apparatus, etc. Ribbons, bead curtains, netting, sari material, strips of foil, feathers all stimulate the senses as you pass through them.

Spread it

Spread one or more of these on a table or floor - sandpaper, bubble wrap, netting, carpet, plastic sheet. Get the children to feel them or walk across them in bare feet. Talk about contrasts and similarities - smooth, bumpy, soft, hard, cold, scratchy.

Sort it

A basket of natural materials - nuts, large seeds, cones, twigs, bark, feathers, leaves and stones - will stimulate talk as children feel and sort them.

Feel it

Try some barefoot experiences on fake grass, bubble wrap, netting, coconut matting, foil, fleece. Add a blindfold and see what they can tell you then.

Snuggle it

Collect some soft fabrics - fleece, wool, blanket, brushed cotton, fur fabric, lace, silk - and contrast them with plastic, leather, foil, raincoat material, rubber. Talk about comfort and about protection, about 'fitness for purpose.'

Long & short

Collect a basket of ribbons, lace, cord, string and braid. Use this for sorting, talking, waving, describing. Glue it on to card or print with it. Get the children to decorate themselves and their world with it. Or try some weaving on a big outdoor weaving frame.

Markings

Markings on the ground or the walls are sometimes frowned upon! However, they do give children opportunities to have a personal, though temporary effect on their environment.

Playground chalk, markers, spray bottles, aerosols (adults only!), as well as stencils, stick ons and paint can transform an outdoor space, even if it is shared with others.

Use markers and markings as ways to create interest, limit some activities, give suggestions and directions and create environments.

Trails and games can provide interest with little additional equipment.

Check before you start on the permanence of the materials you use - you may not want it to last forever.

Follow it!

Lines, footprints, spots and dots in wiggles, circles, spirals, and curves encourage motor control and changing direction.
Try some right angle turns and dead ends as well as leading children to places of interest.

Counting

Games such as hopscotch, stepping stones, footprints, snakes, with and without numbers or letters. These provide opportunities for counting on and back, finding letters, hopping and jumping with both feet.

Directions

Arrows, signs, pictures and words all give directions - to secret places, treasures or the latest feature of interest.
Try using stencils and sprays for quick signs.

Walls

Hang notices and write signs and instructions - 'this way', 'new today', 'visit our...'
White or black-board paint patches on walls make good chalk boards.

Road and rail

Roads and railway lines for ride-on toys are fun for everyone. Add some pedestrian crossings, lights and crossroads for added interest, and a place for the traffic police or signalman. Build platforms for stations and put chairs for waiting for the bus.

Small world

Chalk and paint are good ways of adding a new twist to small world play. Give the children some chalk to make their own roadway, airport, train track, farm, zoo or dinosaur kingdom.
Make bridges and ponds, crossings and car parks.

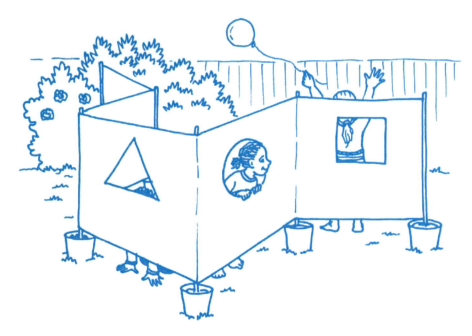

Boundaries & dividers

However big or small your outside play area, it can be made more welcoming by using permanent or temporary dividers and boundaries. These help children to manage their play without interfering with other activities.

All play areas need noisy and quiet spaces, spaces for active play and places for reading, thinking and talking.

We have included here some ideas of how you might make screens, boundaries and dividers in your outside play area. Some need fund raising or involvement of parents and others, some are quick, cheap, easy and temporary.

Whichever you go for, and you may want both, spend some time watching the children first, so you get an idea of the best places to put dividers, and always give them a chance to make suggestions and help with construction.

Living things

Grow hedges and bushes in permanent beds or in planters. Grow vines, ivy, sweet peas in pots placed against trellis for them to climb. Make wigwams of bean sticks and grow beans, flowers or tomatoes up these or in grow bags.

Bricks & mortar

Low walls, grass mounds, path edging and low fences will all help to define areas and some also provide seating. Higher walls and fences should be properly built and could have windows, mirrors, picture frames, glass bricks, coloured glass, etc.

For today

Chalk or painted lines, ropes, bricks, cones, boxes and trolleys can all be used to make temporary dividers on hard or grass surfaces.

Hangings

If you have two or more uprights you can suspend a rope or bar between them. Hang bead curtains, strings, fringing, feathers, fabrics to make temporary dividers.

Cheap & cheerful

A clothes airer, roll of cardboard or some plastic netting can provide a cheap and effective boundary. Unstick a big carton and use the card, or hang a sheet from a rope between two uprights. A line of chairs or tables can work too.

Poles & screening

Set some broom handles in buckets or big tins of concrete, When the concrete is set, use two or more to make screens by clipping or nailing trellis, fabric, card, bamboo screening, plastic sheet or hardboard to the broom handles.

Gardening

Children get great pleasure from growing plants, from digging, planting, weeding and watering. All these activities contribute to personal and social development as well as to knowledge and understanding of the world.

You don't need a garden to encourage children to be gardeners. Most plants will grow in tubs, hanging baskets and pots, and many will grow on window sills and window boxes.

Seeds and pips from fruit cost nothing, garden flower seeds cost little and cuttings, transplants and other ways of propagating will interest and entertain. Collect safe seeds and other fruits on walks and outings.

Containers are cheap and your rooms are always warm, so all you need is some compost or garden soil and a watering can to make a greener environment for the children.

**Check which seeds and plants are safe to use with children.

Tools & equipment

Small hand tools for gardening (trowels, forks, rakes, spades) are not cheap, but if you buy quality they will last. If you are short of money look for tough and durable plastic tools. Add some baskets, watering cans, carpet samples to kneel on, and aprons.

Tubs & baskets

Plants will grow in most containers - plastic cartons, baskets, bowls, tyres, boxes, buckets, tins. Just make sure they have a drainage hole. Most will hang up or sit on a window sill. Try making some window boxes, but fix them securely!

Food seeds

Encourage children to save seeds and pips from fruit (orange, guava, avocado, apple), and vegetables (carrot tops, sprouting potatoes, marrow, pepper).

Bulbs

Plant some bulbs in the autumn, outdoors or indoors, and watch them grow through the winter. Plant outdoor bulbs near the windows or in tubs and window boxes.

In the ground

If you are lucky and have a garden, the children can grow flowers, fruit and vegetables, seeing the whole life cycle of plants and enjoying the results. Involve parents in helping to care for the garden during the holidays.

Fast growers

If you want to see quick results, try these - sunflowers against a sunny wall, tomato plants in a grow bag, runner beans up canes in a wigwam shape. Nasturtiums, morning glory and canary creeper give quick blooms, and a 'mile a minute' or Russian vine will cover a shed in no time!

See The Little Book of Growing Things for more gardening ideas.

Weather

Every day is different. We know the effect that weather has on children's behaviour and our own feelings. Use all the opportunities that the weather brings to have fun outside. Except during extremely cold weather, you should try to make outdoor play available every day. We all know how children respond to being cooped up, and our feelings about outside duty should not affect their entitlement to be outside!

It is always wise to inform parents that children need suitable outdoor clothing every day, even if they come to school by car. You may also want to collect extra wellingtons, gloves and hats so you are ready for everything the weather can bring. Children need shade from the sun, and most settings now advise the wearing of sunhats, and many provide shade for activities in summer.

In the wind

Try wind socks, windmills, streamer ribbons, mobiles, wind chimes, kites, feathers, floaty fabrics, fake long 'hair', flags and banners, bubbles, balloons, paint blowing, leaf catching. Do washing and drying. Go running and racing.

Raindrops

Have umbrellas, buckets, tubes and pipesready for the rain. Use stretched plastic 'drums' to hear the rain. Have raindrop races down the windows, drop oil in puddles, go puddle jumping, use rain gauges and funnels, look for snails, play rain sticks.

Words

Collect and display weather words - hot, cold, splash, blow, wet, drip, fall, float, drop, fly, soaking, freezing, melting, evaporating, shining, reflecting, etc.

Charts

Make an outdoor weather chart. Use waterproof pens on a white plastic sheet, or use velcro 'grab tabs' on a backing, or hang symbol labels on hooks on a board.

Frost, ice & snow

Take every chance to experience snow! Catch snowflakes on hands, clothes, faces. Make angels by lying in the snow. Look at flakes through magnifying glasses. Make snowmen. Ice and frost give other opportunities to look closely and investigate changes as they melt.

Sunshine

In sun or shade, make use of the weather. Make sundials. Grow sunflowers. Watch water dry and ice melt in the heat of the sun. Make sunshades and sunglasses with different colour gels. Hang prisms and mirrors to reflect the light (use plastic mirrors if you can).

Art in the garden

Art activities can be much more exciting in the garden. They can be messier, bigger, noisier, more physical than those indoors.

Everything you do indoors can be done bigger and with their whole bodies. Cut paper bigger, use bigger brushes and markers, leave activities out for longer. Use whole bodies for painting. Do big bubble prints, use huge sponges - spray, pour, blow, drip and squeeze paint. Use clay, collage and dough for group projects. Experience clay. plaster, sand etc. with feet, hands, fingers. Use natural objects to make pictures, patterns and prints. Sew and weave on a big scale.

We have made suggestions for some permanent additions to your outside area as well as some activities that you might select from day to day.

The Little Book of Outdoor Play

Fixtures

Screw a wooden batten to the wall so you can pin up paper or card for painting. Screw some boards to the fence for chalk and painting. Make these big, so that groups of children can work on the same picture. Paint a square of blackboard paint on a wall for pictures.

Painting

Offer water to 'paint' the building, the bikes, the shed. Fill plastic spray bottles with runny paint and paint on paper or the fence. Use rolls of lining paper for long paintings in groups. Paint on the windows. Try using sheets of plastic for see-through pictures.

You & me

Make opportunities for children to work together on tables, walls or the ground. Discuss the activities and how to do them together. Give the children choices of where and when to do things.

Think big

Leave huge sheets of paper up or on the ground all day to encourage returning to the picture. Use decorator's rollers and big brushes. Glue on the sheets things you find outside.

Hands on

Offer finger painting, hand and foot printing. Use big quantities of dough, gloop, slime, cooked or dry pasta. Feel big blocks of ice, walk on sand or gravel. Try plaster casting. Drive bikes and prams through paint and over paper. Make big group collages and 'cut and stick' pictures.

Natural materials

Have a scavenger hunt to find natural materials - leaves, stones, sticks - that are in season. Sandwich these between sticky backed plastic and hang in the window or make mobiles, nature strings or collages. Make a weaving frame and weave grass, leaves, sticks, feathers, etc.

Animals & minibeasts

Use your outdoor area for science and personal development by watching birds, animals and minibeasts. Even settings in cities have wildlife in their grounds, although we may have to look more carefully to find it.

Children should be helped to understand the needs of animals, minibeasts and birds, and to take care of them whether they are wild or pets. Gardening will help to attract wildlife in country and city. You may need to buy a book to help you identify the creatures you (and they) find.

Worms, ants, snails and slugs can be kept for short times in suitable habitats, so the children can watch them over time, while respecting the animals' rights to survive!

**Local authorities give guidance on keeping pets, ask for a copy.

Pets

Many settings keep animals or fish. Rabbits, guinea pigs and goldfish are suited to living in your outside area. Pets give children opportunities to watch and sometimes handle living things, to look after them and perhaps take them home for short periods.

Minibeasts

Flower beds, paths, stones and bricks will often yield insects, snails, slugs, ladybirds, caterpillars, greenfly, beetles, spiders and many more. Offer pooters, and magnifiers. Use clear plastic pots, boxes and aquariums to avoid over-handling.

Butterflies

Plant a buddleia or other flowering shrubs in pots or in the garden to attract butterflies. Then watch out for their caterpillars and pupae.

Birds

Make a bird table or a bird bath in a quiet part of the garden. Put a seat nearby so that the children can watch quietly. Hang up bird feeders in winter.

Digging

Digging is a favourite way of finding minibeasts. Worms, beetles, centipedes and others will be exposed. Keep some worms for a while in a wormery made in an aquarium full of soil. Put leaves and grass on the surface and watch them disappear underground.

Natural habitats

A pile of logs in a quiet corner makes a good habitat for wildlife. You may attract snails, beetles, hibernating creatures or, if you're lucky, even a hedgehog.
Move the logs carefully and replace them in order, so you don't disturb the inhabitants.

Writing outside

Plan opportunities for writing outside whenever possible. The outdoor environment, role play, bricks, sand, water, etc., all give stimuli for writing (particularly for active children, who may not choose to write or make marks indoors).

When you plan your week, it is useful to consider where you could make links between the planning for other activities, indoors and out, and these opportunities for writing.

Children should have free access to mark-making materials outside, as well as adult initiated opportunities.

A trolley, basket or box of materials should be available every time they go outside, and role play areas should include opportunities to write in role.

Materials

Some suggestions: pens, clipboards, pencils, chalk, crayons, card for notices, sticky labels, badges, arrows. You'll also need string for signs, big felt pens, paper of different sizes and types (including forms), staplers, sellotape, a hole punch.

Labels and signs

Some things to start children off: put signs on sheds and play houses; label activities by picture or word; hang labels on hooks, door handles; make badges for yourself and others.

Model the use of clipboards, signs and notebooks.

Letters

A table where children can write messages to each other is just as inspiring outside. Add a postbox or a series of plastic pockets to put them in.

Boards

Consider having a notice board, white board, big blackboard, pinboards for pictures and notices, a gallery for messages, a score board.

Role play links

Make sure that role play outside has links to writing. Offer clipboards, lists, phone books, order forms, stamps and envelopes, badges, door numbers, chalk boards, menus, posters, magazines, booking forms, phone books, message pads.

What's the score?

A game outside gives children the opportunity to invent their own scoring systems. Offer them blackboards or clipboards, with chalk or big pens. Or you could make a more permanent bigger score board. Watch how they record.

See The Little Book of Props for Writing for more ideas to encourage writing and mark making.

Sounds

Not only is the outside somewhere to hear sounds, it is somewhere to make them!

Children need opportunities to explore sounds, music with instruments and their bodies. Start with their bodies, hands, feet, mouths. Then they need to add instruments. Found objects and natural materials are good to start with, then some simple percussion, perhaps on a trolley or in a basket.

Don't forget to take the tape recorder or radio outside sometimes (with or without headphones) and remember to give opportunities to explore wind, water and rain to expand their repertoire. Go on a listening walk.

Hang some things from trees, fences and roofs to make the outside different. Find or make a band leader's hat and have a marching band or concert.

Body rhythms

Clapping, stamping, chanting, waving, jumping, hopping, tapping - to taped or radio music, songs or rhymes, or just as rhythms. Play 'Simon Says' or another copycat game with a leader and followers. Use hands to beat on legs arms and bodies.

Wind & weather

Make or buy wind chimes (you can use shells on strings). Make spinners, clickers and windmills. Blow across bottles and down tubes. Hang tubes in the wind. Use rain or other water to make music in tins, on trays, down tubes and pipes. Buy a rain stick.

Technology

Offer music on personal stereos. Turn on the radio for dancing. Tape record sounds outside and play a 'guess the sound' game with pictures.

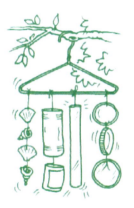

Hang it

Hang saucepan lids, tin cans, tubes, metal tops on strings from trees, fences and walls. Make sound mobiles, from lids and tins. Put up strings of bells.

Make music

Empty cans, bottles, saucepans, bowls and trays all make good drums. Wooden spoons make simple beaters. Bottle tops nailed on a stick make rattles. Also try strings of milk tops or plastic lids. Use dried beans, pasta, peas or gravel in bottles to make shakers.

Instruments

Percussion - bells, claves, drums, castanets, triangles, tabors and tambourines, sticks, sandpaper blocks, rattles, shakers, bongos, cymbals.
Tuned - chime bars, xylophones, tubular bells.
Wind - recorders, whistles, pipes, toy trumpets.

See The Little Book of Music & The Little Book of Junk Music for more ideas for music making – indoors and out.

Construction

Construction in the garden is not just big bricks; it's science and technology, buildings, structures, challenges, shelters, bridges, tunnels and so much more.

Take the big bricks outside, and try some new things as well. If your children are ambitious, you will have to keep an eye on safety.

Found items can be even more exciting than things from catalogues. Just make sure they are clean and free from rust, nails and splinters. Ask parents and friends to help you find stuff for big construction. You may have a parent with connections - they may even do the maintenance for you.

Encourage children to work collaboratively and teach them good safety habits as they work.

Bridging & joining

Planks, ladders, poles and ropes can be used to join fixed and temporary structures. Solid boxes or crates with handles will make good supports for bridges, slides and walkways. Use them to make shop counters or seats too.

Found things

Tyres, inner tubes, rope, string, bricks, wood, big tins and tubs, cardboard and plastic tubes, carpet offcuts, fabric - all these will bring new elements to play.
Be sure to check them before use to make sure they are clean and safe.

Joining

Provide clips, fabric strips, velcro, string, rope, elastic, parcel and duct tape. Offer them in a basket or on a trolley, so children have access to work out their own solutions.

Flat pieces

Use, for example, card from boxes or cartons, sheets of plywood, corrugated card in sheets or rolls, carpet, blankets, stiff plastic sheeting, bubble wrap.

Science & Technology

Have available tubes, buckets and baskets, funnels, guttering, pulleys, wheels, hose pipes, siphons, lids, cogs, chutes and ramps. Magnifiers, mirrors (plastic), magnets. 'Phones' can be made from tins and string. Pipes and funnels, soft wire, cord, tape and glue will be useful, too.

Poles & screens

Set some broom handles in buckets or big tins of concrete. When the concrete has set, use two or more to make screens by tieing or nailing trellis, fabric, card, bamboo screening, plastic sheet or hardboard to the broom handles.

Quiet areas

The outdoor area should not just be for messy and noisy play. All children need to be quiet sometimes, and they should be able to find somewhere outside to be still and reflective, to chat to an adult or friends, to read a book, to look closely at a flower, leaf or insect, or just to rest from the busy activity of the day and enjoy the garden.

These quiet places can be temporary or permanent. They all need to be comfortable, welcoming and clear in purpose, so they are not invaded by children who want or need to be more active. Providing a quiet area is important at all times of the year and in all weathers.

Safety tip: you will need to think about protection from the elements (sun, wind, cold) as the children will be moving less and therefore more at risk of chilling or sunburn.

Seating

Use picnic chairs with an umbrella, a wooden garden seat or bench, pub garden style picnic tables, swing seats, bean bags low walls, blankets. Make sure there are some places for friends to sit together, or for an adult and child to share.

Screens & boundaries

Hedges and other growing plants give green screening. Trellis, net, clear plastic and fencing give a view from both sides. Low walls, paths, cones and lines can mark temporary boundaries. Furniture brought out from inside can also be used.

Protection

Use sunshades, gazebos, awnings and parasols in summer. Screens of bamboo, willow, shrubs in pots, umbrellas, and wind-breaks all have uses in cold or wet weather.

Listening

Make a photo book of the things you can see and hear in a quiet place. Use this for listening and spotting. Offer headphones and story tapes outside.

Activities

Almost anything you do indoors can be brought outdoors for use in a quiet area - books, puzzles, sewing, collage, letter writing, puppets, card games, listening to tapes.
Try mirrors and magnifiers, small world play or small construction for a change.

Nature watch

Quiet areas are perfect places for having bird tables and feeders, small ponds and wildlife sanctuaries. Hang streamers, and quiet bells and wind chimes. Offer binoculars, beetle boxes, cameras and spotter's guides. Hang a weather chart.

Role play situations

Role play outside can be even more fun. There is plenty of space for several situations, linked or separate. You can arrange water in the teapots, rides and walks, places to push the baby's pram, and opportunities to direct the traffic, go upstairs, run for the bus, deliver letters, go to several shops or visit the quiet area for a sit down in peace.

If role play situations relate to each other - a house and shop, a baby clinic and a chemist, a house and a barbecue - the role play will become much more complex and the children will have so much more fun!

Out of doors you can also give free rein to children's own ideas, either by providing a choice of prop boxes or by encouraging them to invent their own places and situations, using fixed apparatus or construction.

Fixed features

Build a simple wooden house feature in a corner or against a wall. Cut holes for windows and a door. Or make a castle, tree house, or cottage. You can buy a ready made house, shop or a shed specially for role play, but home made ones are often more fun.

Temporary features

Put up tents. Or get a huge cardboard box & cut out doors and windows. Make your climbing frame or slide into a castle or pirate ship for the day. Make a train or bus with chairs or planks. Use a table for a shop counter or simply make some hats for role play.

Huts & sheds

When all the toys are out and your shed is empty, use it for a role play corner, a play house or a garage. Put a table across the doorway to make a shop or cafe.

Baskets

Put a different basket outside containing just one or two role play items each day: for example, a hat and badge, a tabard and whistle, a bird book and binoculars

Situations

Here are some situations which have been successful out of doors. You will be able to think of many more!

a parcel office	a plant centre
a window cleaner	a garage
a car wash	a drive in restaurant
a plane with attendants	a newsagent with deliveries
a bike hire shop	a library
a row of houses	a farm or zoo
a fete or a gymkhana	a lighthouse
a picnic	a camp site with little tents
a sports day	a market

See The Little Book of Role Play for more role play ideas.

Surprises

Surprises in the garden stimulate play, revive old ideas and lend a sense of fun. Children will enjoy looking for the surprises, and you will enjoy thinking them up!

Of course, as with the indoors, you want the outdoor environment to have a sense of order and stability, but small surprises help the play along and may give a little guidance to those children who are either withdrawn and needing support, or to those who have so much energy they need a bit of 'channelling'.

Surprises can be anywhere and in any form. They can be visible or hidden, in writing, signs or objects. They can take the form of equipment in unusual places or combinations. They can give children an opportunity to look at or use things in a new way. Here are some ideas to start you off.

Safety tip: use only plastic mirrors

The Little Book of Outdoor Play

Signs & notices

Put signs on role play areas (shop names, 'Mr Gumpy lives here', Ice cream today, Car Wash, etc). Put signs on poles (arrows, STOP, No through road, One way only, No bikes, Park here, etc.) Stencil footprints to follow. Stick pictures on the wheeled toys (fire truck, pizza bike).

Light, shadow, reflection

Put battery powered lights in tents and tunnels. Pin paper to a wall or spread on the ground, so the sun makes shadows of children and objects. Suspend a mirror in the roof of a tunnel or other shelter, in the quiet area or on the ground. Hang prisms and mirrors in trees or from lines.

Find it!

Hide small world people or other toys in the garden and have a toy hunt. Hide small objects and have a treasure hunt. Have a challenge - 'Find a stone like this, a leaf like this' etc.

Inside outside

Take some of the indoors out - a dolls house, playmat, jumping stands. Put Lego and playdough together outside. Put games and puzzles under an awning or on a blanket. Have a story outside.

Baskets

Fill a small basket with new objects or familiar things in new combinations. Try a basket of cones or shells, some seeds, small balls, big chalk and small world or cars, ribbons on short sticks, scissors, card and big pens, magnifying glasses, magnets, a personal stereo, bubbles.

Suspension

Hang up some feathers, leaves, sequins, beads and mirrors*. Tie ribbons on apparatus and bushes. Hang hoops or picture frames for children to climb through. Put out washing lines hung with clothes or soft toys. Have a hammock or a swing in a tree.

The Little Book of Outdoor Play

Small apparatus

Fine and gross motor skills can be developed in the garden or outside area as well as in the hall or indoor space, and most settings have a collection of small apparatus. You can expand the selection or the use of these by some simple additions. Of course, depending on the age of the children, the balance between more formal games and free play will differ, but all children enjoy handling and manipulating, throwing and catching, running and jumping with this equipment.

Some settings have different types of small apparatus available on different days or at different times of the year. Other settings have a trolley, labelled with pictures, so apparatus can be chosen and put away by the children.

The Little Book of Outdoor Play

Throw, catch & Kick

Try to offer balls of different types and sizes - footballs, plastic & sponge balls, beach balls, bean bags, quoits, rubber balls. Suggest and model how to use them for kicking, throwing, catching, dribbling. Add some bats for hitting. Use cones for markers and goals. Place buckets and hang hoops for aiming.

Jumping

Mark small circles or footprints with chalk or paint for jumping (put them in patterns, so some are for both feet, some for one). Set up low canes and cones to jump over. Mark parallel lines as rivers or roads to jump. Practise skipping with short or long ropes.

Running

Provide markers or cones for running, weaving and dodging, or as finishing posts. Use wrist or arm bands for simple catch. Offer ribbons or streamers for a change.

Markings

Paint or chalk targets on fences, walls and ground. Arrows for following, wiggly and straight lines, footprints, number lines, hopscotches, marble runs and skittle alleys. Roll coins and marbles or flip counters.

Brushes & rollers

Fine motor skills can be helped by using tools in the garden. Try decorators brushes and water to 'paint' the walls, toys and equipment. Use rollers, sponges or spray bottles on big sheets of paper or plastic. Offer big pens and chalk for signs and notices. Try clipboards and markers for outdoor drawing.

More ideas

Try skimmers, balloons and boomerangs. Fix a blanket down with pegs or bricks to crawl under. Use big tubes or boxes to join large apparatus. Use planks and poles for hanging and balancing. Make or buy some stilts. Or with the children, make an obstacle race using all the equipment.

Permanent structures

Many of you are working in settings where the outside area is difficult to manage, shared, subject to invasion from outside, or non-existent. Many settings are short of funds and cannot rely on sponsorship from parents or local business. In these situations, you might consider making some of the ideas portable or put them on wheels or trolleys to make them movable.

However, permanent outdoor shelters and structures can be part of the outside environment in many settings. Financial and physical help can be available from local firms, parents, charities or fund raising events.

Here are some ideas for those more permanent structures. Local builders, garden centres, DIY shops and businesses may be able to add their support to staff and parents in the setting.

*Plant list on pages 50 to 54

Screens & dividers

Some suggestions - living willow, planted in a dividing bed; glass bricks let light through but still give privacy; walls with holes in to look or climb through, also set with mirrors or picture frames; wicker, bamboo or trellis fencing provides a place for plants* to climb.

Raised beds

Raised beds for plants* (e.g. vegetables, herbs or shrubs) give them protection from feet and wheeled toys. They also make islands in concrete or asphalt areas. If they are at the right height, children can garden standing up. Use sleepers, bricks, tyres or metal tubes.

Tracks

Tracks for cars and trains can be a permanent feature - either on a raised area or at ground level. Mould cement to make track, platforms, hills, slopes. Add markings with gloss paint.

Role play

Make a 3 sided construction against a wall, using marine plywood or fencing. Add a door and window. Screw a blackboard on the door so you can change the focus or write a notice.

Quiet areas

A willow or wicker canopy or shelter, with a built in seat; a 3 sided fence with seating, on grass or asphalt; a tower or tree house with a ladder and space for parking underneath; a hammock frame or swing seat; a sunken garden area with grass and flowers (for the really ambitious!)

Sensory areas

You only need a few pots or tubs to make a small sensory garden. Fill them with some herbs and scented flowers (see page 50 for ideas). If you really want to go to town, add raised beds, water features, decking, a range of surfaces at ground and higher levels, wind chimes and streamers.

Access for all children

The ideas in this book are for all settings and all children. However, there are some children who have additional needs and need special support.

The Early Years Foundation Stage guidance states that all children have a right to outdoor play, whatever their circumstances, background, difficulties or disabilities. Children with special needs also have a right to play "both inside and outside".

Here are some ideas and points to consider in order to ensure access for all children to the experiences of the garden. You will have more, and may want to get in touch with us to share these, perhaps in another Little Book!

On page 52 you will find a list of shrubs, plants and seeds which are suitable for young children to grow and care for.

Physical mobility

Children in wheelchairs, buggies or frames need plenty of room if they are to gain independence. Check doorways, steps and other spaces. Try to offer a range of games and equipment so that children with mobility aids can find something for them. Raise plants and sensory experiences to higher levels.

Visual difficulties

Ensure there are plenty of sounds (chimes, bells, etc.). Check risks of tripping. Make sure visual clues and signs are very clear, using pictures and symbols as well as words. Use a range of small apparatus (bigger balls, brushes, markers), so they can join in.

Allergies...

Check allergies before planting. Be aware of the seasons, when the pollen count is high and when grass is cut. Make sure there is shade and protection from the sun.

...and more

Some children have asthma or eczema. Provide shower caps and gloves for sand and water play, Be careful when using perfumed oils. Set up easy access to inhalers and other medication.

Hearing difficulties

Fix a wooden batten to the wall at about head height. Pin or tape a fabric awning to the batten and tie the ends to two poles to make a simple shelter (see page 49). You can use the shelter as a shop, or to provide shade for table top games, books, sand or bricks.

Behaviour difficulties

Some children have difficulties managing the choices and freedom outdoors. Offer a smaller range of choices at first. Make clear rules and set up systems for sharing. Try a timer for bike use, velcro bracelets or bands to limit on the number of children in an activity.

Boundaries, screens, shelters and plants

Plants are an essential part of the outdoor environment. Boundaries, screens and shelters increase the possibilities for imaginative and investigative play outdoors. The following pages give some ideas for making or otherwise providing some things which will enrich the outdoor experiences of your children.

Boundaries and screens may be natural - for example hedges, bushes, or lines of quick growing climbers in pots or grow bags - or constructed, or a combination of both. Natural boundaries and screens are permanent or semi-permanent. Most contructed boundaries will be movable, and are therefore more versatile. If you make a set of poles or markers from broom handles set in buckets of sand or concrete you can use them for a variety of purposes. Paint them in bright colours, and sling tapes, streamers or fabric between them - or tie trellis to them for something more resilient. Watch out for splinters if you use garden trellis.

A simple but very effective shelter is a sheet or blanket thrown across a rope stretched between two uprights. If you can fix battens to walls you can use them again and again to anchor awnings. About 1.5 metres makes a good length. Treat the batten with wood preservative and give it plenty of time to dry. Fix it to the wall at a height of about 1.25 metres. If you use a weatherproof material such as plastic for the cover you can tape or staple it to another batten and use hinges to fix this to the one mounted on the wall. For something which will need to be taken in out of the rain, fix small curtain rings to the material and hang them on cup hooks screwed into the battens. Make sure that any battens with hooks are high enough to be out of the way of eyes.

At the end of the summer, garden centres will often sell off structures which make excellent ready made shelters - small tents, plastic gazebos and so on. At such times they can be had very cheaply. While in the garden centre you might want to check out the plants for your outdoor area. We have suggested on the following pages a range of plants with various characteristics and for different locations. However, you should tell your supplier where and how you intend to use the plant(s) to ensure they are suitable for what you have in mind. None of the plants we suggest here are poisonous, but you should make sure that children always wash their hands after they have been playing with or around plants - and of course discourage them from eating any plant not provided specifically as food.

Ideas for boundaries and screens

Ideas for shelters

Suggestions for plants and flowers

check with the supplier that the plant
is suitable for the place and purpose you intend.

Climbers
Convolvulus
Ivy
Morning Glory
Honeysuckle
Nasturtium
Hop (Humulus)
Boston Vine (Parthenocissus)
Glory Vine (Vitis Coignetiae)
Sweet peas

Sun lovers
Pinks/carnations(Dianthus)
Aubretia
ice plant (Sedum)
Houseleek(Sempervivum)
Blue lily (Agapanthus)
Pansies
Daisies (Bellis)
Marigolds (Calendula)
Erigeron (daisy flowers)
Geraniums
Helichrysum (everlasting)
Chinese Lantern (Physalis)
Golden Rod (Solidago)
Nasturtium (Tropaeolum)
Verbena
Mesembryanthemum
Achillea (Yarrow)
Montbretia (Crocosmia)
Limnanthes Douglasii
(Poached egg plant)

Shade lovers
Hosta
Ivy
Primula/primrose
Violets
Periwinkle (Vinca)
Dead nettle (Lamium)
Forget me not (Myosotis)
Lady's Mantle (Alchemilla)
Astilbe
Granny's Bonnet
    (Aquilegia)
Bleeding Heart (Dicentra)

Tubs and baskets
Pansies
Alyssum
Busy Lizzie (Impatiens)
Petunia
Marigold (Tagetes)
Begonia
Harebell (Campanula)
Lobelia
Mimulus
Viola
Lobelia

Fast growers

Morning Glory
Nasturtium
Sweet peas
Sunflowers
Busy Lizzie (Impatiens)
Nasturtium (Tropaeolum)
Golden Hop (Humulus)
Boston Vine (Parthenocissus)
Glory Vine (Vitis Coignetiae)

Ground dwellers

Periwinkle (Vinca)
Anthemis (Chamomile)
Thyme (Thymus)
Candytuft (Iberis)
Speedwell (Veronica)
Hardy geranium
Rock rose (Helianthemum)
Ground cover roses (Rosa)

Evergreen/Winter interest

Grasses
Cyclamen
Heathers
Myrtle (Myrtus)
Flax (Phormium)

Perfumed foliage

Myrtle (Myrtus)
Pelargoniums
Choysia

Perfumed flowers

Pinks (Dianthus)
Alyssum
Wallflowers

Bulbs

Crocus
Snowdrops
Hyacinth
Small daffodils
Grape hyacinth (Muscari)

Everlasting flowers

Straw flower (Bracteantha)
Limonium
Love in a mist (Nigella)
Helichrysum
Chinese Lantern (Physalis)

Or you could sow some
wild flower seeds in a
patch of grass which is
left longer than the rest.

Suggestions for <u>shrubs</u>

check with the supplier that the plant
is suitable for the place and purpose you intend.

Climbers
Convolvulus
Ivy
Morning Glory
Wisteria
Thornless Blackberry
Cotoneaster horizontalis
Honeysuckle
Passion flower (Passiflora)

Sun lovers
Lavender
Berberis
Wygela
Shade lovers
Hydrangea
St John's Wort (Hypericum)
Spiraea

Perfumed foliage
Eucalyptus

Perfumed flowers
Lavender
Philodelphus
Daphne
Wisteria
Lilac (Syringa)

Fast growers
Morning Glory
Kerria (grows anywhere)

Spiny or prickly
Holly
Mahonia
Pyrocanthus
Gorse (Ulex)

Screening
Cotoneaster (prickly!)
Box (Buxus)
Forsythia
Lavender (Lavandula)
Currant (Ribes)
Lonerica
Black bamboo (Phyllostachis)
Striped bamboo (Pleioblastus)

Evergreen/Winter interest
Cornus (Red stems)
Choysia
Some clematis
Eucalyptus
Yucca
Hazel (Corylus)
Tassel Bush (Garrya Eliptica)
Willow (Salix)
Viburnum

Trees
Birch (Betula)
Rowan (Sorbus)
Crab apple (Malus)
Plum and cherry (Prunus)

Flowering
Butterfly bush (Buddleia)
Ceanothus (Blue)
Hebe (low growing)
Prunus (flowering)

Berries
Cotoneaster horizontalis
Hawthorn (Crataegus)
Holly (Ilex)
Firethorn (Pyracantha)
Rowan (Sorbus)

The Little Book of Outdoor Play

Suggestions for indoor plants

check with the supplier that the plant
is suitable for the place and purpose you intend.

Indoor plants (foliage)

Climbers and trailers
Philodendron
Ivy (Hedera)
Inch plant (Tradescantia)
Vines (Cissus)

Bottle gardens and terrariums
Begonia rex (small leaved)
Ferns
Peperomia
small ivy (Hedera helix)
Maranta
Ficus pumila
Dracaena
Saxifraga

Survivors!
Aspidistra
Spotted laurel (Aucuba)
Asparagus Fern
Spider plant (Chlorophytum)
Coleus
Castor Oil plant (Fatsia
    Japonica)
Ivy tree (Fatshedra)
Fig (Ficus)
Mother in law's tongue
    (Sansevieria)
Succulents of all types
Jade plant
Inch plant (Tradescantia)
Cacti

Umbrella Plant (Cyperus)
Baby's Tears (Helxine)

Something unusual
Bryophyllum - little plantlets
    grow on the edges of
    the leaves
String of beads
Living Stones (Lithops)

Indoor plants (flowering)

Climbers and trailers
Bell flower (Campanula)
Ivy leaved Geranium
    (Pelargonium)
Bead plant (Nertera)

Survivors!
Shrimp plant (Begonia
    Beloperone)
Wax plant (Hoya)
Busy Lizzie (Impatiens)
Flaming Katy (Kalanchoe)
Geranium (Pelargonium)
Peace lily (Spathyphillum)
Christmas pepper (Capsicum)
Winter cherry (Solanum)
Christmas or Easter Cactus

Bulbs
Small forms of garden bulbs
Amaryllis (Hippeastrum)

The Little Book of Outdoor Play

Suggestions for food plants

check with the supplier that the plant
is suitable for the place and purpose you intend.

Climbers
Thornless blackberry
Tomato
French/runner beans, peas
Marrows, squashes,
    cucumbers, courgettes
Or try a grape vine!

Sun lovers
Sage (Salvia officinalis)
Nasturtium (Tropaeolum)
Onions (Allium)
Garlic
Most herbs

Tubs and pots
Try small varieties of apples
and pears (make sure
you have a self fertile
type, or plant two).
Strawberries grow well in
    tubs or pots
French or runner beans,
    peas and cucumbers
    grow up sticks or trellis
Tomato plants grow in tubs
    or grow bags
Try ornamental cabbages
Grow potatoes in buckets
Grow basil and parsley **Herbs**
Marjoram (Origanum)
Thyme (Thymus)
Rosemary (Rosemarinus)
Cotton lavender (Santolina)
Lemon thyme (Melissa
    Officinalis)
Mint (Mentha)
Chives

Fennel
Basil
Dill

Fast growers
Carrots
Beans
Lettuce
Marrows
Pumpkins
Radishes
Spinach

Attractive to insects and butterflies
Butterfly bush (Buddleia)
Sedum
Alyssum
Calendula
Dianthus
Myosotis
Solidago
Aster
Ceanothus
Lavender (Lavandula)

Decorative
Kohlrabi
Red cabbage
Ornamental cabbage
Artichokes and cardoons
Alliums, leeks and onions

Indoors
Mustard and cress
Carrot tops
Beans
Pips and seeds from fruit
    and vegetables.

If you have found this book useful you might also like ...

**The Little Book of
Growing Things**
LB22
ISBN 1-904187-68-4

**The Little Book of
Outside in All Weathers**
LB17
ISBN 1-904187-57-9

**The Little Book of
Playground Games**
LB30
ISBN 1-904187-89-7

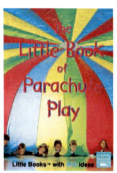

**The Little Book of
Parachute Play**
LB24
ISBN 1-904187-80-3

All available from

Featherstone Education   PO Box 6350

Lutterworth LE17 6ZA

T:0185 888 1212   F:0185 888 1360

on our web site

www.featherstone.uk.com

and from selected
book suppliers

The Little Books Club

Little Books meet the need for exciting and practical activities which are fun to do, address the Early Learning Goals and can be followed in most settings. As one user put it

"When everything else falls apart I know I can reach for a Little Book and things will be fine!"

Little Books Club members receive each <u>new</u> Little Book on approval at a reduced price as soon as it is published.

Examine the book at your leisure. Keep it or return it. You decide.

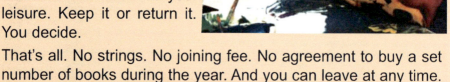

That's all. No strings. No joining fee. No agreement to buy a set number of books during the year. And you can leave at any time.

Little Books Club members receive -

- ♥ *each new Little Book on approval as soon as it's published*
- ♥ *a specially reduced price on that book and on any other Little Books they buy*
- ♥ *a regular, free newsletter dealing with club news and aspects of Early Years curriculum and practice*
- ♥ *free postage on anything ordered from our catalogue*
- ♥ *a discount voucher on joining which can be used to buy from our catalogue*
- ♥ *at least one other special offer every month*

There's always something in Little Books to help and inspire you!

Phone 0185 888 1212 for details